Deadly Nightshade & Other Poisons...

Andrea Dean Van Scoyoc

Nightshade   Van Scoyoc

First Edition: 2024
Rs. 200/-

Cyberwit.net
HIG 45 Kaushambi Kunj, Kalindipuram
Allahabad - 211011 (U.P.) India
http://www.cyberwit.net
E-mail: info@cyberwit.net

All work within this poetry/short ghost story publication, is a work of pure fiction, crafted by the author's darkly inspired mind.

Any semblance to anything other than what this work is intended to be, a trip into the darker side of the soul, is pure coincidence and must be treated as such.

Printed at Repro India.

Nightshade   Van Scoyoc

Foreword:

Deadly Nightshade (Atropa Belladonna)
elegant, delicate...deadly.

Like many other things in life, beauty...
with a high price attached.

I love deadly flowers. I always have.
Proof of what many of us know about,
but overlook in life...

Our existence is both cruel, kind, caring,
hateful, a wonder...and a bane.

Therefore, with that in mind, each poem
and story in this book is prefaced by a
chapter dedicated to a deadly plant or
flower.

I hope you enjoy your trip into my
darkly pretty, but woeful world...

~Andrea Dean Van Scoyoc

Nightshade   Van Scoyoc

Nightshade   Van Scoyoc

Chapter One

Belladonna

In autumn's hue, the leaves do fade
A somber sight, upon the shade
Of gravestones, where the dead do lay
Their final rest, in endless gray

The fallen leaves, like tears they fall
A sorrowful reflection, the completion
of all
The lives that once did thrive and grow
Now but a memory, in tow

The marble slabs a steadfast stand
Against the wind and time's demand
Enduring through the seasons' sway
A testament to life's brief stay

The leaves, they whisper, as they fade
A soft goodbye, to those who've made
Their final journey, to the grave
Their legacy, forever they crave

The ancient stones, a silent guard
Of memories, that will never blur
A poignant reminder, of life's short span
A call to cherish, each moment, as best
you can...

Nightshade   Van Scoyoc

In glades of shade, where shadows dance
and play,
Woe engulfed, a heart's heavy sway,
A burden born, a weight that will not
stay,
A grief so deep, it cannot fade away.

The wind whispers truth, a gentle
breeze,
A soothing balm, a fleeting ease,
But like a wave, the pain returns anew,
A sorrow's tide, that will not subdue.

Nightshade   Van Scoyoc

The stars above, they twinkle bright,
A celestial show, a wondrous sight,
But in their light, a shadow falls,
A sorrow's stain, that screams its call.

The moon, a silver crescent smile,
A beacon of hope, a guiding light,
But even she, cannot soothe the pain,
A sorrow's grip, that wields its might.

The world outside, a busy throng,
A din of noise, a never-ending song,
But in the midst, when hearts do break,
A sorrow's moan, that will not shake.

Nightshade   Van Scoyoc

In fields of sorrow, wretched tears flow
Cry until you die, let your heart be low
The pain of life will never cease
Tears fall like rain, like a never-ending
breeze
Your eyes will stream with sorrow's stain
A quiet sigh, let your heart remain

The weight of grief will never fade
Tears are a dark cloud, a reminder of
mistakes we have made
In this world of hurt we have no choice,
Abandon all zeal, your life has no voice,

The ache of loss, all we can do is try to
deal
Tears fall like winter snow, a wound that
will never heal.

Nightshade   Van Scoyoc

Whispers at night, a gentle breeze
Carrying secrets, no one can seize
Softly spoken words, a lover's plea
In the darkness, only we can see

The stars up high twinkling so bright
As our hearts beat fast, lost in sight
The moon, a silver glow
Illuminates our love, as it grows

The wind whispers truth, a gentle voice
Telling us of a tricky choice
To follow dreams, to make them real
Or hide in fear, to never feel

Nightshade   Van Scoyoc

The night air cools, the dawn breaks
through
A new day starts, a fresh point of view

The whispers fade, the silence stays
But the love we share, it never fades
away.

Nightshade					Van Scoyoc

In dusky vales the ghosts of yore
Haunt the realms of days gone by
Their whispers echo through the night
As they sing a mournful dirge and cry

Their footsteps tread the ancient stones
That mark the passage of their lives
Their pleas and sobs, the echoes of their
moans
Resound through endless strife

Their forms, a wisp of mist and smoke
They fade into the darkness deep
Yet in the shadows, they do speak
Their secrets, in the sleep

Their eyes, like lanterns in the night
Glow with sorrow and with pain
For they have seen the end of light
And know the darkness will remain

Their hearts, like Fall's decayed leaves
They wither and they fade
Yet in their hallowed chambers
They rue the the spirits they could not
save

Nightshade   Van Scoyoc

Their voices, like the wind
They hiss through skeletal trees
Their stories, like a winter's chill
Carried like fears upon a breeze.

Beneath the moon's pale glow,
a spectral forest lies motionless...still,
Where dead trees stand, their limbs
outstretched, brandishing their will
To live and thrive, long since lost in time
Their bark is rough, their leaves all
shriveled
Dead long before their prime.

Nightshade   Van Scoyoc

Their once-vibrant colors now dulled,
their life force dwindled nigh
The wind still whispers through,
a pained and mournful sigh,
As if it spoke of days gone by, and
memories once true.

The stars above shed a tear,
For in this place, where life once
flourished, now lies a silent fear.

The pale trees stand, a haunting sight,
Their beauty marred by time's
unyielding might.
Their limbs creak and groan in ghostly
sound,
Echoes of a life once full, now lost
profound.

But in their death, a beauty can be
found,
A testament to life's fleeting, ephemeral
sound.
For even in decay, there's still a grace,
A reminder of the cycles of life's
embrace.

Nightshade   Van Scoyoc

So let us cherish these dead trees, and
the tales they tell,

Of lives once lived, and gentleness oft
felt, and hearts once lovingly swelled.

For in their silence, we may hear a voice,
A call to cherish each day, and to make
the most of life's long road
A never ending choice.

Nightshade   Van Scoyoc

Nightshade   Van Scoyoc

Chapter Two

Angel's Trumpet

Dinner with the dead, a macabre feast
In a graveyard, where the departed rest
The tables set with seats of stone,
Tombs of the forgotten names long
gone.

The ghosts of the past, they gather
round
Their voices hushed, their eyes cast
down.
They share tales of lives long since past
And the memories that will forever last

The aroma of decay, it fills the air
As the dead savor each bite with care
The flavors of the rotted, so rich and
bold
A culinary delight, best served cold

The wine, a vintage from the crypt
below
A taste of the soil, so dark and slow
It flows like blood, as the night draws
sour
A dinner party, which grows eerier by
the hour.

Nightshade   Van Scoyoc

The moon, a glowing orb in the sky
Casts shadows on the tombstones high
A night of revelry, a dinner with the
dead
Where for only a few hours, no more
tears are shed.

In fields of green, where once lay the
dead,
Now empty graves, devoid of dread,
Their occupants risen, their souls set
free,
In a world beyond, where they'll always
be.

Their final resting places, once so still,
Now echo with the laughter of their will,

Nightshade   Van Scoyoc

Their memories kept alive, in the hearts
that knew,
Their love and joy, forever true.

The graves, once marked with stones so
gray,
Now blanketed with wildflowers' sway,
Their beauty blooming, like aurora's
first light,
In this world of wonder, within endless
night.

Their stories told, their legacies kept,
In the memories of those who wept,
Their love and kindness, never to fade,
In the hearts of those who knew them
from dawn to shade.

Nightshade   Van Scoyoc

In shadowed gardens where darkness
plays.
Where ebon's cold heart staves off the
day,
A deadly beauty blooms beyond
compare
Poison flowers, their petals so fair.

Their colors are vibrant, a wicked toxin
exudes,
In the moonlight, they seem to gleam
anew.
But take careful heed, their charm is a
snare,
For in their touch, death lurks so
beware!

Their scent is sweet, a siren's call,

Nightshade   Van Scoyoc

Lures in the unsuspecting, one and all,
But those who dare to drink their brew,
Shall suffer a fate, most cruel and true.

Their thorns so sharp, a deadly embrace,
Their venom courses in a long and fatal
race,
A slow and painful death, they bring,
To those who dare, their beauty to cling.

So take care, the lethal flowers of night,
Their beauty and their power, a
wondrous sight.
For in their depths, lurks a sorrowful
rue,
That once shared...there's nothing one
can do.

Nightshade   Van Scoyoc

In fields of gold, where once we'd stray,
Our love now lies, as dead as day.
The sun that shone, the flowers that
sway,
No longer bring us joy, but dismay.

The laughter we shared, the tears we'd
dry,
Are now but memories, passing by.
The warmth of touch, the sweetest kiss,
Are but a distant, fading bliss.

The wind that whispers through the
trees,
The rustling leaves, the birds at ease,
No longer bring us peace, but pain,
As our dead love remains, in vain.

But the stars still twinkle in the sky,
The moon that glows, hopelessness is
nigh,
No longer bring us hope, but fear,
As our dead love casts its gloom only
here.

Nightshade   Van Scoyoc

The world continues to spin round,
The seasons come, as time winds down,
But our love, twill never will be found,
For it is dead and lost to the lonely
ground.

Nightshade   Van Scoyoc

Chapter Three

Monksbane

In twilight's hush, the forest weeps,
For lost secrets no longer to keep.
Her laughter flowed like a lovely bird's
cry,
As warm as the sun, as clear as the sky.

Her eyes were like stars and shone so
bright,
And in their depths, did joy take flight.
Her touch, like summer's warmth, did
bring,
Comfort to all who heard her sing.

The wind softly whispered through the
trees,
A sorrowful melody, in the form of a
breeze.
For she, who brought us such joy and
light,
Is gone and lives now within the night.

The once lovely flowers droop their
heads,

Nightshade   Van Scoyoc

In mourning for her now she is dead,
The birds, they sing a sorrowful song,
For her, who made their hearts so
strong.

The sun in grief hides its face,
In shame, for taking her away,
Leaving us in the endless dark,
And sorrow, no more words to say.

Nightshade   Van Scoyoc

In misty morn, a garden fair,
With gothic spires and statues rare,
Guard as sentinels, they silently stand,
From prying eyes...this is *their* land,

Flowers bloom here like delicate lace,
Are as dark and mysterious as shadowed
grace,
Woven from the dank of night,
And borrowed from the moon's pale,
light.

The trees are like giants, high and
strong,
Their limbs entwined like gnarled tongs,
An embrace in gloom, an ashen cast,
Enhance this Potter's Field of past.

The air is heavy with the scent of night,

Nightshade					Van Scoyoc

And the distant howling of a lonesome
beast,
That haunt this gothic garden's bite,
And keep the living from the feast.

Yet, in this twilight garden's heart,
A secret lies, a treasure to impart,
Within beauty that shines ever so bright,
And brings salvation back to light.

Nightshade   Van Scoyoc

In slumber soft, death does lie,
A gentle embrace, a saddened sigh,
The end of pain, the end of strife,
A peaceful rest, the close of life.

The angels sing, the heavens smile,
Gone away to sleep if only for a while,
As souls depart, their trial and toil,
In eternity's sweet arms, they rest in the
soil.

The grave, a quiet, still embrace,
A final resting sacred space,
Where weary hearts go to eternal rest,
And weary bones find solace blessed.

Death, a mercy, a release from pain,
A respite from life's tempestuous reign,
A time to repose, a time to heal,

Nightshade   Van Scoyoc

Sweet and peaceful always, a final gentle
yield.

In fields of the forlorn, where sunsets
ebb and fade,
Lies a tale of angels, tainted by the
mistakes they made.
Their wings, were pure as snow, now
gray,
With rust and rot, and edged with decay.

Their halos, at one time, a shining
crown,
Now tarnished and dull, with sin's dark
frown.

Nightshade   Van Scoyoc

Their voices, once a sweet and heavenly
sound,
Now hoarse and grating as the acrid
ground.
They danced and sang, in days of old,
But now they wander, lost and cold.
Their hearts no longer full of grace,
Now an empty and bitter space.

No longer winged, swift and free,
Now weighed down by the weight of
decree.
Their beauty, once a shining light,
Now faded, lost in endless night.

Their facades of bliss now lost to shade,
Filled with hatred of the errors they've
made,
Hearts filled with love and cheer,
Now empty and lost in endless fear.

But still they dance, in fields of gold,
Their movements, now tarnished, slow
and old.
Their shining eyes merely dull and dim,
Their voices, once sweet, now saddened
and grim.

Nightshade   Van Scoyoc

In twisted temptation, the devil's mark
A sign of darkness, a burning spark
A brand of evil, a token of sin
A taint that haunts, a never ending
wound begins

It glows with embers a burning desire
A flame that lures, a passion of fire
A scar that corrupts, a soul that's lost
A price that's paid, at too high a cost.

The devil's mark, a sign of shame
A brand that marks, a life's lost name
A symbol of power, a token of might

Nightshade   Van Scoyoc

A tattoo that's feared, a scream in the
night.

It whispers sweet nothings, a succubus
call
A promise of pleasure, a danger that
enthralls
A tear that's etched, a heart that's sealed
A fate that's reviled, a soul that's revealed

The devil's grin, a sign of doom
A brand that damns a life to gloom
This sum of evil, a price that's paid
A scratch that's eternal and a soul that is
stained.

Nightshade   Van Scoyoc

A storm is coming, not comforting or
mild,
With winds that howl and thunder that's
wild.
The skies are dark, the clouds are black
Walk away quickly and don't look back

The rain pounds down, like a thousand
drums,
As the wind whispers secrets, of a world
undone.
The lightning flashes, like a dancer's
grace,
And the thunder rolls, with a mighty
pace.

The trees sway and creak, like a lover's
embrace,
As the storm rages on, with a fierce, wild
face.
The waves crash and roar, like a beast
awake,
While the world is bathed in a wild, wet
lake.

Nightshade   Van Scoyoc

The storm is here, it's a force so grand,
A display of power, in this wild land.
It brings us life, and it brings us strife,
A reminder of nature's wild and
untamed life.

Nightshade   Van Scoyoc

In the dead of night, when the world is
still,
The midnight thunder rolls, a madman's
thrill.
The sky is angry, the wind is cold,
As tortured souls gather, their power to
unfold.

Their roar is like a stormy sea,
As they ride the wind, wild and free.
Their laughter echoes through the night,
As they dance with glee, a wicked sight.

Their eyes glow bright, like burning
coals,
As they conjure up their darkest souls.
Their power is immense, their might is
great,
As they unleash their fury, a demon's
hate.
The thunder crashes, the lightning
flashes,
As the spirits revel in their midnight
splashes.

Nightshade   Van Scoyoc

Their roar is deafening, their strength
supreme
As they wreak unholy havoc, whispers to
a scream.

But as the sun begins to rise,
The phantoms flee and their power dies.
The sky clears, the wind subsides,
And the world is quiet, the storms now
hide.

Until the next night, when they'll return,
To unleash their fury, to burn and yearn.
For the midnight thunder of awesome
power, tis a never-ending quest,
To bring chaos and terror, to a world at
rest.

Nightshade   Van Scoyoc

In solemn dusk's hush, where shadows
play,
Amidst the trees, forms of darkness
sway,
A raven, deadly as the night, they say
With eyes like coal, bow your head and
pray.

His plumage glistens, like the moon so
bright,
But do not be deceived by his fair sight,
For in his heart, a darkness dwells,
A malevolent force, that none can tell.

He glides with grace, his wings are wide,
And in his beak, a secret he does hide,
A deadly toxin, he is the spirit of death,
And with one glance, hope is lost in
breath.

His eyes are like lanterns, shining bright,
Reflection of fear, as his presence takes
flight,
For all who see him, tremble with fright,

Nightshade   Van Scoyoc

For they know, the raven's touch is a
deadly might.

So if you see him, in the darkened skies
Do not approach, avoid his eyes
For the raven's power, is a force of pain
And his touch is fatal...you'll never be
seen again.

Nightshade   Van Scoyoc

In midnight's hush, a figure appears,
A harbinger of death, of dark and drear.
The wind will cry and the trees will
sway,
As fate's dark messenger comes to stay.

Her wings, like blackest night are spread,
A shroud of doom, a final dread.
Her eyes, like voided depths so low,
A glimpse into the abyss below.

With each grim step, the ground will
shake,
A tremor inside and your soul will break.
Flowers will wither and the trees will
fade,
As death's dark shadow each spirit she
invades.

The air becomes thick and heavy with
fear,
As one by one, the living disappear.
The harbinger of death, a grim delight,
A final reckoning, a darkest night.

Nightshade   Van Scoyoc

Death's cold hand, so icy and grim,
Reaches out to claim what's left of him,
A fragile form, once full of light,
Now but a shadow of its former sight.

The breath of death, so hopeless and
mean
Extinguishes the spark that once did
gleam,
And in its place, a darkness deep and
wide,
Consumes the soul, and all its pride.

A heart, once full of hope and song,
Now beats no more, its rhythm gone,
The once bright eyes, now dull and dim,
Can no longer see...only a shade of him

Nightshade   Van Scoyoc

His body, once so full of grace,
Now limp and still, a lifeless trace,
A memory lost in a fleeting storm
Now bitterness and agony are the only
norm.

The cold hand of death, so cruel and
tight,
Squeezed him hard, with all its might,
No more the warmth of sunshine bright,
Just darkness, and engulfing fright.

In a land of perdition, no sun to light the
way,
Lies a body, cold and gray.
No dream is left, no brightness to stay,
Death's icy grip took him home today.

The sun hides its face, a veil of night,
The stars weep tears of distant light.
The wind whispers secrets of the past,
As his body's life force finally died at
last.
The moon, a silver crescent smile,
Illuminates the final, treacherous mile.
The grass, a soft and mournful hue,

Nightshade   Van Scoyoc

Beneath the weight of death, so true.

Her world will now become a canvas of
despair,
A painting of hopelessness too much to
bear.

Her heart, a heavy burden of care,
A weight that cannot be shared.
His corpse is shriveled, stiff and still,
A victim of fate's cruel will.
His soul to wander, lost and alone,
In search of a forever, peaceful home.

Nightshade   Van Scoyoc

Chapter Four

Foxglove

In the hushed stillness of the moonlit night, the ancient mausoleum stood sentinel among the overgrown graves, its crumbling stone facade kissed by time.

A chill lingered in the air, swirling with whispers of forgotten tales, and from within the cold, shadowy depths emerged a vision both haunting and beautiful: a woman, ethereal in form, with cascading waves of silken hair that danced around her shoulders like strands of spun silver.

Her garments, tattered yet exquisite, fluttered as if caught in a gentle breeze, revealing glimpses of her translucent skin that glowed with a luminescent radiance, a striking contrast to the darkened graveyard.

Nightshade   Van Scoyoc

She was the embodiment of lost love, a spirit bound by longing, seeking the embrace of the one who had stolen her heart in life, now lost to the chasms of death.

With each graceful step, the ground beneath her bare feet stirred, as if recognizing the gravity of her sorrowful quest, her sapphire eyes shimmering with unshed tears that caught the moonlight like stars fallen from the sky.

She drifted past tombstones etched with the names of the forgotten, her heartache echoing in the stillness as she called out softly into the night, each whisper laced with desperation and hope.

The fragrance of wilting roses, remnants of love offered long ago, weighed heavy in the air, guiding her as she navigated the pathways of loss.

In a world caught between life and the afterlife, she could feel his presence

Nightshade   Van Scoyoc

lingering like a shadow, a distant
heartbeat that pulsed through the
contorted branches of the trees, urging
her onward, weaving her between the
realms of the living and the dead.

With every flicker of her ghostly form,
she longed for their reunion, an eternal
dance through time and space, where
the boundaries of existence blurred, and
the promise of true love beckoned her to
the edge of mortality, a desperate
journey ignited by an everlasting bond
that even death could not sever.

Nightshade   Van Scoyoc

In a forlorn and forgotten mansion...ravaged by the cruelty of passing and wretched woe...decaying in an ancient forest where the moonlight barely pierced through the tangled branches, a ghostly woman roamed.

Ethereal and hauntingly beautiful, her figure shimmering in the shadows like a wisp of smoke caught in an eternal dance, her sighs nothing more but whispers in shadows.

Each night, as the darkness thickened and silence cloaked the land, she would ascend to the lonely rooftop that overlooked a vast, cursed abyss, tethered to her tragic fate—a spectral figure bound by the chains of betrayal.

Her hair, long and flowing like silken threads of midnight, framed a sorrowful

Nightshade   Van Scoyoc

visage adorned with tears that
glimmered like starlight in the dark.

With every haunting hiss of the wind,
she called out the name of the man who
had shattered her heart, a name that
echoed in the solemnity, reverberating
through the trees and engulfing the
silence—a name that brought both
agony and a flicker of forgotten love.

As the first light of dawn threatened the
grip of night, she would prepare herself
for the ritual that bound her to this grim
tableau; looping a noose of spectral rope
around her neck, she would take one last
shuddering breath of the cool night air,
her heart heavy with the weight of
memories and the sting of being cast
aside for another.

With a final, anguished cry, she would
plunge into the fading shade, only to
awaken anew at twilight, her beautiful
form forever shackled to the void,
damning her to relive those fateful
moments as she hung in phantom

Nightshade   Van Scoyoc

suspension, desperately calling for him,
wanting to know why he forsook her,
why he let his heart wander.

The cycle repeated endlessly, each night
a reflection of her pain, each dawn a
reminder of her unresolved fury,
neither life nor death able to release her
from the clutches of a love transformed
into a lament—forever haunting the
living and cursing herself, a tragic
melody against the backdrop of a
timelessness...eternity.

Nightshade   Van Scoyoc

As the sun dipped below the horizon, casting a golden hue over the tranquil waves, a handsome, ghostly figure emerged on the rocky shore, his ethereal presence both chilling and captivating.

Dressed in a tattered suit of centuries gone by, he settled himself upon the jagged stones, the soft sound of crashing waves harmonizing with the melancholy notes that slipped from his ornate violin.

The bow glided expertly across the strings, producing a haunting melody that broke through the blackness, laden with a profound sadness that tugged at the hearts of those fortunate enough to hear.

Each night, as the stars began to twinkle in the vast blanket of the night sky, the

Nightshade   Van Scoyoc

ghostly man became the embodiment of longing, his sorrowful eyes searching the stormy horizon as moonlight bathed him in ghostly splendor.

He poured his soul into each haunting note, as the story...as old as any of the old folk could remember...of his sorrow, lamenting a love lost to a life cut short in the dawn of her days, brought those too entranced to move...to tears.

As he played, his translucent cheeks wet with agony, created small, glistening trails that reflected the light of the moon.

Locals rarely spoke of him, but when they did, it was always in hushed whispers of the spectral musician, weaving tales of longing and loss.

Though the exact story of how he came to be had been forgotten...even to the oldest of the town archives, he was feared, he was avoided on "those nights"

Nightshade   Van Scoyoc

the sky took on "that" color...and yet...he was admired.

Some claimed he was the spirit of a shipwrecked sailor, forever bound to this desolate shore, while others believed he was a forgotten artist, cursed to play his mournful tunes until he found the peace that eluded him in life.

Each performance felt timeless; the music transcended the ordinary, touching the very essence of the human experience, evoking emotions that resonated deep within the soul.

And so, on those special nights, he played on—a forever fable of memory and heartache, weaving his sorrow into the fabric of the night, a poignant reminder of the love stories that linger long after their echoes fade, encapsulated for eternity in the mournful strains of a ghostly violin.

Nightshade   Van Scoyoc

By the light of a large bright full moon,
giggles pierced the moonlit
luminescence of the cemetery.

As shadows swirled and spoke secrets to
the night, a little girl with tousled hair
and a dress made of threadbare
patchwork held the delicate hand of a
rotted ghost child as they played
between the weathered gravestones,

Nightshade   Van Scoyoc

their laughter echoing like a lullaby through the stillness of the air.

The moon bathed the scene in an otherworldly light, illuminating the ancient and intricate carvings on the headstones, where names and dates faded into obscurity, each one bearing witness to a life once lived.

Unfazed by the eerie surroundings, the unwanted and neglected human child twirled around, her voice a sweet symphony as she asked the ghost child questions filled with innocent curiosity, eager to know what it felt like to drift among the stars, or whether she ever missed the warmth of the sun on her face.

The ghost, in her rotted lace dress that seemed to flutter in a breeze that no one could feel, her hollow eyes and tattered skin giving away an age of long ago, responded with a gentle smile, a gesture that seemed to transcend the boundaries of life and death, weaving a tapestry of

Nightshade   Van Scoyoc

companionship that defied the dreariness of their surroundings.

They played hide and seek among the stones, their songs ringing out through the silence, while they skipped silently behind a crumbling mausoleum, the air heavy with the scent of damp earth and the faintest hint of decay.

In their spectral playground, the little girl felt no fear, only the enchanting thrill of friendship, her heart unburdened by the weighty realities of mortality.

She shared dreams of adventure and stories of princesses and magical lands, while the ghost child offered her the lore of the bygones of her day and of her own, now eternal, existence.

The lonely human child wrapped herself in the mysteries of a time she could never know, tinged with a hint of sadness as her phantom friend related

Nightshade   Van Scoyoc

the fleeting moments of joy that once
filled her tragically short life.
Under the luminous gaze of the moon,
with stars twinkling like scattered
diamonds, the two children...their souls
forged in an unbreakable bond, enjoyed
a fleeting connection that turned the
graveyard into a realm of imagination
and play.
Love, loss, and laughter mingled into an
unforgettable midnight symphony,
echoing through the hallowed ground
until the morning light.

As the crescent moon rose higher into
the velvet black sky, the graveyard
transformed into a lover's gathering

Nightshade   Van Scoyoc

where spirits swayed among the ancient gravestones, and the air was thick with an otherworldly charm.

In a secluded corner, overlooking a gentle slope lined with wilted roses that had long since surrendered to time, sat a beautiful zombie couple, their decayed yet enchanting features illuminated in the ethereal light.

They were an unlikely sight, with tattered remnants of what once were elegant evening attire: the gentleman wore a frayed tuxedo, his head barely holding a battered top hat; what was left of a dried rose pinned to his pocket, while the lady was festooned in a tattered red gown, delicate strands of moss weaving through her hair like a crown of nature's splendor.

The couple, though lifeless, emanated an undeniable aura of love and tranquility, their empty eye sockets while holding no expression, stared solely at one another as they lingered over a delicate

Nightshade   Van Scoyoc

porcelain tea set, beautiful, but terribly
ravaged by time.

The sloshing tea, a thick, loamy brew,
released a faint aroma of dank that
mingled with the scent of damp soil and
fading petals, creating a macabre and
tragic atmosphere.

With every sip, they exchanged amusing
tales of their former lives, their laughter
echoing through the graves as if
breathing life back into the chilled night
air.

A ghostly breeze swept through the
potter's field rustling the leaves
overhead and causing the lanterns they
had placed around them to flicker like
stars come to life.

In that moment, they were not just souls
joined forever to the past; they were
vibrant, living memories, each moment
filled with warmth and companionship
that transcended even the boundaries of
death.

Nightshade   Van Scoyoc

Time lost its meaning as they toasted their undying love, the clink of their cracked teacups resonating like a melodic bell, a testament to a bond that refused to fade away, not even in the stillness of the graveyard at midnight.

The wind howled in anguish, as if feeling the bitterness of abandonment in the forlorn cemetery.

The passage of time had been terribly unkind as it rendered many of the

Nightshade   Van Scoyoc

gravestones nearly unrecognizable beneath a veil of moss and lichen.

There, a solemn wind that rampaged as if driven by an unseen giant, grasped angrily at the solitary figure standing with a raven perched delicately on his shoulder.

Clad in a tattered coat that seemed to absorb the silence of the place, he moved with a quiet determination, his bony fingers working diligently at the stone surfaces, brushing away the green fuzz that clung stubbornly to names and dates long since faded from memory.

The raven, its glossy black feathers glinting in the dappled sunlight that filtered through the gnarled branches overhead, watched with an almost sentient awareness, its beady eyes reflecting an ancient wisdom that seemed to echo the sorrows entangled in the very fabric of the cemetery.

Nightshade   Van Scoyoc

Each gravestone he tended told a story, whispered in the gentle rustle of the leaves that surrounded him, and with every swipe of his hand, he felt an odd connection to the souls that lay beneath, as if he were giving them a voice once more.

The air was thick with the scent of earth, decay, and the lingering fragrance of wildflowers that stubbornly sprouted amidst the tombstones, creating an oasis of color in a realm dominated by shadows.

He often found that his thoughts drifted to the lives these stones represented—a mother lost too soon, a soldier fallen far from home, a child taken before understanding the world—but he pressed on, guided by an intrinsic belief that he was honoring their memories, in each clearing of the cold, green coating an act of reverence.

The evening light began to fade, casting long shadows that reared up from the

Nightshade   Van Scoyoc

ground, and as he stood back to admire
his work, he felt a sense of solitude wash
over him, yet he was **so** alone.
It was a poignant kind of peace—a silent
communion between man, nature, and
the forgotten souls resting in a world
that had moved on without them, a
reminder that even in desolation, there
can be beauty and purpose.

Nightshade   Van Scoyoc

~Author Bio:~

Tragic, misunderstood and decidedly different, master Poetess and Storyteller, Andrea Dean Van Scoyoc has led an enviable life, fraught with broken dreams, pain and empty shores.

But within disappointment and pain, she has found a purpose...a way to share her sorrows...her poison pen.

For more of Andrea's varied works, visit her official website:

https://linktr.ee/theandreadeanvanscoyoc

Nightshade   Van Scoyoc